T0072571

Dear Hubby,

About Your Retirement

A Guide for Staying at Home

NANCY ROBISON

FIRESIDE
Rockefeller Center
1230 Avenue of the Americas
New York, NY 10020

FIRESIDE and colophon are registered
trademarks of Simon & Schuster, Inc.

For information about special discounts
for bulk purchases, please contact
Simon & Schuster Special Sales:
1-800-456-6798 or
business@simonandschuster.com

Designed by Barbara M. Bachman

Manufactured in the
United States of America

1 3 5 7 9 10 8 6 4 2

Library of Congress
Cataloging-in-Publication Data is available.

ISBN 0-684-85196-2

Many thanks to my friends for
your interest, encouragement, and
input for this book. Requests have
come from wives whose husbands
are about to retire, as well as from
those who have just retired,
to include helpful information
on this transition in their lives.
I hope this answers some
of your questions.

DEAR HUBBY,
ABOUT YOUR RETIREMENT

Other books by
NANCY ROBISON

Dear Daughter, About Your Baby

Dear Son, About Your Baby

Dear Daughter, About Your Wedding

Dear Son, About Your Wedding

A FIRESIDE BOOK

Published by Simon & Schuster

NEW YORK   LONDON
TORONTO   SYDNEY
SINGAPORE

DEAR HUBBY,

*W*ell, the day we've both been waiting for is just about here. And believe me, I am looking forward to it as much as you are. No more alarm clocks! No more starched shirts! No more suit and tie! No more packed lunches, unless, of course, it is for a fun picnic together!

I've missed your company over these past many years. While we both had careers and were raising a family, we hardly had time for each other. When we got hitched—if you can remember back that far—we were the best of friends.

Each day, I looked forward to you coming home in the evenings and spending the few precious hours together before sleep time, then it was up at the crack of dawn and another day started all over again. Now we can pick up again where we left off before those busy, busy days. Just one of the perks will be traveling off-season and missing the crowds, as well as getting a better bargain. Also we can have neighbors and friends in for dinner and cards; go to the movies mid-week or to the matinee, which is less crowded. Dining out midweek will be less crowded too. Sounds good, doesn't it?

Retirement will be quite a change, but nothing to fear.

People dream about retirement. They wonder what it will be like to not have a daily schedule. Some fear it. But it can be looked at as a new adventure, rather than something to dread. Think back to your first day of school or the first day of work. You had shaky knees, felt afraid, but soon adjusted—didn't you? Well now, this time you won't have to do it alone. We have each other, and we can face this together.

Long days ahead might look daunting. It doesn't have to be scary.

We will soon get reacquainted in our new relationship, and start a new routine. You have spent so much time away from home and on

the job that your coworkers probably know you better than I do.
Being together only a few hours
each day will change into 24/7
(that is, twenty-four hours, seven
days a week, as our plumber says).

EXPECT TO MAKE AN
ADJUSTMENT IN YOUR
MENTAL ATTITUDE

So, it will be enjoyable for us both to see whom we are married to! Maybe we'll stay up later and sleep in a bit longer in the mornings. I hope so. But we should agree to rise and shine each day with new expectations of things to do. I say "we" because your retirement certainly affects me—even though I might keep my part-time job—and, of course, there's always the housework to do.

Expect to make an adjustment in your mental attitude. If you're dreading retirement, you may be miserable. But if you're like Bob, who took twenty minutes to adjust and has loved retirement ever since (for the past ten years), then you'll be fine.

I hope you don't have to go through an identity crisis wondering who you are. It may be hard when you are no longer the boss or the head cheese. Not that I'm going to boss *you* around . . . very much (at least I'll try not to). Or, if you're retiring from your old boss and you can set your own schedule without anyone telling you what to do.

At first we may want to spend all our time together, but remember the old adage, "Absence makes the heart grow fonder."

Now don't you worry about keeping busy. There are plenty of things to occupy both body and mind. There's no doubt about it. Surely, there will be adjustments to make, but it's important to keep busy, to stay committed to daily living, not just occasionally. But if you have a mind set against this adjustment and say, "I don't want to do anything!" then we've got a problem. At first we may think every day is a holiday, but that will wear off and we'll have to get serious about what to do *every* day. We'll need some kind of a plan of action to make our days interesting and active. Retiring from *all* activity "blahs the brain and mushes the body," says one of our friends.

You don't need to have an identity crisis—a "who am I?"-type of thing—just because you don't have to drive somewhere to work anymore. You may worry that there may be long days looming ahead. But fear not. It doesn't have to be. Take it easy. Have fun. Enjoy!

First of all, remember that you are not retiring from life. Just from a job. But you must find things to fill up your day. As a friend of yours said, "There's nothing wrong with retirement, as long as you don't stop working!" Another friend gave these words of wisdom: "Retirement does not mean stop or quit living, but just start a new lifestyle!" I'm sure you will agree once you've rested enough, played plenty, and caught up with all the things you've always wanted to do.

Retirement is not necessarily related to age. Recently someone in

PLAN OF ACTION

our circle said, "Yesterday is gone; forget it. Tomorrow never comes, because when it does, it's today." We know a few forty-year-olds who have made their fortune, or enough, to retire early. Then there's

Rory, who has never worked—very much. He just gets by on money earned from being a part-time fence mender and house painter— but he couldn't be happier.

Age has nothing to do with retirement. Remember when we went to your fiftieth class reunion? Everyone was approximately the same age, but you felt years younger than anyone there—except for Coach Carlson, and his darling little petite wife, who put everyone to shame. He was eighty-five years young. And I do mean it. He and his wife looked younger than many of the students—or, I should say, attendees of the reunion. My point being, young or old is a state of mind. Being retired does not mean you're over the hill or can't do things that you like. Remember that. It's important.

Do you remember when prizes were given out for the ones married the longest and the ones with the most children? Remember the couple that hobbled up to get their prize for being married fifty-two years (they were married in high school)? She looked very old and drab and he too looked all worn out. Of course, nobody judged them until the next prize winner got up, the same age, but looking trim, happy and smiling, a very gracious woman who had had nine children—five boys and four girls. The drab woman, sitting in front of us, gave this classic remark to her husband: "Well, some people just preserve better than others!" So if we have a choice, let's be well preserved.

Take Mac, for instance, who in

his eighties goes around the world—Russia, South America, Africa—helping to train farmers to market and distribute their fruits. He makes long trips up and down

the Amazon River in Brazil. This, of course, is not for everyone, but Mac has the resources, know-how, and desire to help others. Charitable giving keeps him young and active.

WHEN YOU ARE RETIRED YOU WILL HAVE TIME TO ENJOY LIFE

At a recent U.S. Open tennis match, some of the "old-timers" were playing in the senior division, for those fifty-five and over. After interviewing some of the players in their late sixties, the young commentator said, "Wow! I hope I'm still playing tennis when I'm sixty-five!" Well, kiddo, every day you will find eighty-five-year-olds still hitting and placing the tennis ball so well that it doesn't matter a twit that they "don't have wheels" (can't run). Their putaway shots twist, turn, drop, lob, and hit the line for winners. *Life does not stop when you retire from your job.* Your job is/was just a means to an end. When you are retired you will have time to enjoy life—enjoy being at home. And you will probably not relax as much as you think. Yes, the first year or two you will, but then boredom might set in. What will you do next?

There are tons of useful and fun things you can still do and literally mountains to climb. You have a lifetime ahead of you. Today's life expectancy has increased fifty percent from what it was a half century ago. Think of it! Remember the number of octogenarians and centenarians we know. Take Helen, for instance, who is in her mid-nineties and walks ten blocks each morning to get her newspaper, and another half mile in the afternoon for her lunch. Remember what she said

ENJOY BEING AT HOME

when asked why she didn't have her paper delivered? "How would I get my exercise then? If you just keep moving, you won't die!" We know a half dozen of these people with this vital attitude. No longer are so-called senior citizens feeble. You don't have to, nor will you want to, just sit around and wait for the end. So you can get that out of your mind right now. It's a new beginning, Sweetheart! We should celebrate! We're starting over!

Budget

It will be necessary to write up a tentative retirement budget. You know, we've lived with a budget all our married lives, so this won't be difficult. Of course, we'll continue this planning, taking care to live

within our means, our pension, etc. We must cover food, house payments, travel, recreation, and health care. And as well as we can, set aside a portion of our income for contingencies (including insurance and maintenance).

Remember, a budget is just a *plan* we can use to anticipate the myriad details we must deal with day by day. It is not at all set in

**YOUNG OR OLD
IS A STATE OF MIND**

concrete. We can adjust it as things change, as they surely do.

Rules

There are some written rules, somewhere, about retirement and the things you should and should not do. I don't agree with all of them. Some caution against selling your home and moving away from friends. Well, there is merit in that for some; however, I see it a little differently. We are starting out on a whole new adventure, a new phase of our life together, and I think we should start anew—make a change. (However, it would not be wise to sell *everything* and make a move without doing thor-

ough research into our prospec-
tive new digs. And I have heard
some say that they have resisted a
change, then later after having
made it, just loved it. It works the
other way too. So, we shouldn't be
hasty, but it is something to think
about.)

Consider This

Since you do not have any hobbies
to keep you in one place, why
don't we sell the house, sell the
furniture (except for the special
stuff) and begin again? We could
move to a new location, away from
the city, where there is better
weather, more activity and action.
Not only will there be things for

you to do, but we *both* will be getting a new start.

You see, our home has been my office and workplace all these years. It is where I do my daily work, like cook, clean the house, make the beds, wash and iron the clothes, care for the garden, deal with the workmen, the mail carrier, and the telephone calls, get gas in the car and take care of getting it repaired, do the care for the children, etc Believe me, running a house is much like running a small business—only it is another 24/7 job— with me as the CEO, the secretary, treasurer, *and* working staff. You will be coming home to *my* office! You won't want to follow me around any more than I want to follow you around. So, when you come home, do not try to change things to fit your habits. It would be like me retiring and moving into *your* office or workplace. You wouldn't want me to rearrange your office, would you? I have a certain place for everything and a schedule that I follow weekly, just like you had at your job. Now with you home all day, every day, this will change—and rightfully so. I have no complaints. Let's do it together. You can probably do some of my old chores better than I can! (But please, don't rearrange my sewing basket or my makeup drawer! If it really bothers you, tell me, and I'll do it!)

The funny thing is, housewives generally don't retire. They still plan three meals a day, do the laundry and the ironing, make the beds, write checks, do banking, and so forth, as I said before. But now, Dear Heart, you can help!

Not that I'm a fussy housekeeper. However, one of the things you, my dear, have liked is coming home from work to a clean, neat house. Now that you will be home every day, you can *help* to keep it that way by tidying up after yourself. I am your wife, not your maid. I say this with love; I will help you, but not wait on you. Now that you will be home most of the time, let's not change this arrangement. You can certainly help keep it that way by running the vacuum once a week, washing windows, keeping the patios swept and washed, and other things I'm sure you'll think of.

And while you are outside, you can:

- *water the plants*
- *trim the shrubs*
- *rake the leaves*

- *empty the trash and put out the barrels on trash pickup day*
- *keep the barrels clean and lined with trash bags*
- *keep cars clean and waxed*
- *tidy the garage*
- *tie up newspapers*
- *arrange tools and garden tools separately*
- *mark and store Christmas boxes, travel information, photos*
- *tend to and file important papers*

Oh, my, I'm getting carried away and don't mean to scare you. Let me take it a little easier.

I know you will want to read

the newspaper every day, either in print or online.

And you'll want exercise, of course. How about some sports? Golf, tennis, lawn bowling, cycling, walking, jogging, racquetball, surfing, skating, swimming, aerobic workouts, weight lifting, and more.

Why not build a vegetable garden? Not enough room? Try getting a plot at the senior center.

And there are wonderful walks and beautiful drives we can take. And guess what? Finally we'll have time for in-depth conversations.

And at least once a week, we should plan a short day trip—perhaps to the zoo or to smaller com-at have special festival

can go for an overnight or

or the day for a nice getaway.

Think of this—any time we want to!

And remember, you've been threatening to illustrate the history of the world! Now you will have the time.

For a while you will be happy to just relax, and I'm all for it. Perhaps you will want to tackle some home projects. Or work with your model trains, which you have been just itching to do. Or explore new frontiers. But you won't want to sit on the beach and read novels *all* the time. I don't think!

Soon you'll be so busy you'll wonder when you had time to work!

Examples

My suggestion to start fresh, under a new roof, with new boundaries for our desks, computers, tools, supplies, and hobbies, is probably a good one. Besides, we don't need such a large house anymore with the children off on their own.

This may not work for everyone, of course, but it's worth giving it some thought. Some of our friends could never part with their homes, and maybe we can't either. But let's talk about it anyway.

Everyone has a different experience, you know. And if we make a mistake, it's not the end of the world. We'll try something else. For instance, our friends the Johnsons retired to a beach community—a lifelong dream of theirs. But after ten years, they decided they had done everything in the area that they wanted to do, so they sold their home for a nice profit and moved to another location.

Another couple moved from a large house to a smaller one, only to discover there was nowhere to go for privacy except the bathroom. Big mistake! They were soon sharing *everything,* even their space! So consider this when changing homes. You need someplace to read while your spouse is watching television and vice versa.

Mary and Dave sold their home, purchased a motor home, and traveled the country extensively. They were so happy. They could have gone on and lived that way forever—so they thought. But then they got tired of traveling, and had to have a place to return to—a base—and they missed their family. So it's good to think more in the long term, rather than in the short. (Especially if an irreversible financial decision is involved.) Perhaps traveling around for a year or two would be great, and in our travels we might find the perfect valley or paradise where we'll want to settle. Very well and good. But think of our friends, children, and grandchildren, and ask your-

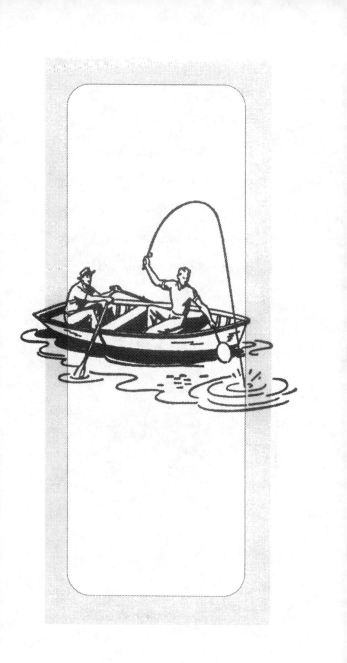

self, "Are we in such a remote spot that they will never come to visit?" Something to consider.

Another couple built their dream house, and guess what? When it was finished, they sold it and moved back to their former neighborhood! It wasn't what they

wanted after all. They said, "We thought we would live here forever. It was our retirement house, but things and ideas change."

Another couple we know sold their home and furniture and moved to another area to have a fresh start. Leaving a much-too-quiet residential area, they found a place with activities constantly going on. They were near theaters, water sports, tennis, and golf; having no hobbies of their own, such as woodworking or model building, they found this area fit their needs. It worked out well for them—and they lived happily ever after.

Each one of us is an individual and must make our own decisions, and whatever it is, it will work out okay. But plan carefully and with an escape plan built in!

Then there are the RV travelers, or, as some say, the "seasonal seniors." We met Ron and Doris at that guest ranch we visited last summer. They were retired but took on the status of migrant workers and traveled from resort to resort doing odd jobs during peak tourist seasons. Sometimes she was a waitress and he a cook. Sometimes they were just official greeters. But they earned enough money to pay for their travels and they loved interacting with other travelers from around the world and having the freedom to do what they wanted. They had also given tours at historical monuments, sold Christmas trees, picked apples, taken tickets and strapped youngsters into rides at theme parks, and cared for private campgrounds across the country.

Another couple found their freedom and fun another way. They joined a team of firefighters as part of the fire camp's staff, supporting the workers with fresh water and food. They are always packed and ready to go when the call comes.

The laid-back, over-the-hill image of older people in rocking chairs sitting on the porch is fading away. There is so much out there for us to do. But I'm not suggesting that this rolling life is for us, my dear; however, it is something to consider. It might be fun to see our country and do a good deed at the same time.

Of course the majority of retirees stay put in their homes, surrounded by familiar territory and friends. But remember, my dear, as I mentioned before, and I may need to say again: if this is the category we stay with, please beware that this is where I cook, clean, wash and iron clothes, care for the garden, deal with the workmen, the mail carrier, and the telephone calls, put gas in the car and take care of getting it repaired, etc. This is my office.

Things to Do

Now I've heard many wives tell their about-to-retire husbands, "I don't do lunch!" Or, "For better or for worse, but not for lunch!" Well, with me it's different. I *do* "do lunch." In fact I'm looking forward to having company—someone to eat with every day. It's not fun eating alone and I can't go out with the girls *every* day! So let's have lunch together at home or out somewhere and we won't have to rush for any reason.

- **There will be places to go, things to do.**

- *There will be time for hobbies and relaxation.*
- *Keep a journal of everyday activities.*
- *Write your memoirs and/or family genealogy or create a family scrapbook (your family will appreciate it someday).*
- *Work for the library in the literacy program, teaching adults to read.*
- *Work for the Friends of the Library, collecting used books for the bookstore or wherever needed.*
- *Work for the halfway house—delivering clothes or donated food from bakeries or markets.*

- *Work for the meals-on-wheels program, taking food to shut-ins.*
- *Work in the day care center.*
- *Work for church—help with maintenance (changing light bulbs, watering the grounds, raking leaves, washing windows, whatever).*
- *Work for the prisons.*
- *Work for the shelters—deliver used clothing to shelters or charities.*
- *Work for the hospitals.*
- *Fix up a home or help out with Habitat for Humanity (along with helping others, you meet new friends—something you might miss by not going into work every day).*

- *Work for the schools.*
- *Teach kids to read.*
- *Tutor your grandkids in reading, math, or whatever, or teach them to play chess.*
- *Volunteer for community services.*
- *Join the neighborhood crime watch.*
- *Go to volunteer police training (help the community in directing traffic, giving directions, or answering questions for lost tourists).*
- *Help in youth programs or sports organizations.*
- *Play cards or read to those unable to get out much.*
- *Take art lessons or a foreign language.*

- *Give lectures or book talks to book clubs.*
- *Manage an apartment house or a building.*
- *Now here's a unique idea: if you like to drive, start an airport service for your friends and neighbors. Offer to drive them to and pick them up from the airport. Give them curb service. They can pay you like a taxi, or if you prefer, just pay for the gas. They'll gladly do it. It's much nicer and more convenient than a taxi or shuttle service, as well as more friendly. What a nice service this is.*
- *Do shopping for shut-ins.*

- *Do small repairs for neigh-bors.*
- *Learn to use a computer and .surf the Net. (Did you know you can play cards with people from all over the world at any time of the day?)*
- *Visit the senior center for more ideas.*

There's so much you/we can do, and through it all don't forget you can rest now and then too!

There are probably thousands of organizations that would welcome your expertise, so there's something to do anytime, anywhere. (Check local papers for numerous volunteer projects.) It's

up to you to make it work—to make
things happen.

Rather than saying why a thing
can't happen, or why something
can't get done, our upbeat friend
Sam is always saying, "Let's *make*

this happen!" There's no reason to
ever have a boring day. But if there
are one or two off days, don't be
concerned. Just enjoy the leisure,
because it won't last. Our grand-

kids will be coming to visit, a neighbor might need his yard watered or papers picked up while away on vacation—or the car might need attention, hair will need cutting, the bushes will need trimming. Or ask yourself, what can I do for someone else today? Wow! That opens up a whole new can of worms!

If you are bored, it's your fault. (Boring is a state of mind, not an irretrievable condition.) There's plenty of activity out there just waiting for you.

Remember Tom? Each day he follows a routine of doing something for the community; something for church; something for the home and wife; and something for himself. He is very productive and feels good about it. And if all else fails, there is the community college or senior center that offers classes in just about anything you want to know about, and you can explore new frontiers.

Even getting another part-time job isn't out of the question—for some. Ted, who is eighty-six,

works at the movie theater taking tickets and loves it. And one of your friends tried retirement for a year and then got another job. He said he was going out to have fun! (To each his own.)

Then, of course, there's the Honey-do list, which can be just about anything from fixing the leaks in the toilet to polishing the brass on the mailbox door.

Retirement does not have to be a nightmare for either of us. You must know you are never under-foot, my dear—however, there *are* some things you can help with, and I'm sure you may have some things for *me* to do too.

Let's Talk About

THE MORNING NEWSPAPER

Read it and dispose of it. Don't leave it open and spread out all over the dining room table all day. If you have something you want to read over again, save it, by all means, but you can fold it, or cut it out and store it at *your* desk, or somewhere by your favorite chair. Half of the newspaper is classified ads anyway. Can't they be taken out immediately? Unless of course, you are scanning them for another job. Heaven forbid!

Coffee

Maybe your office had the coffee maker going all day, but I'm not used to it, so please, clean the pot and put it away after your morning coffee. And please do not leave stale coffee cups sitting around. If you must keep leftover coffee, put a cover on it and store it in the refrigerator for later. Don't leave it sitting around in the living room or on the kitchen counter.

Eyeglasses

Now, here's the story. When you put your glasses in your pocket with your keys and pocketknife, they get scratched or broken. If you refuse to use the cover provided for protection, don't cry about it. (This might get repeated over and over again until you find another place to keep them.)

Smoking

Not many of our friends smoke anymore, but I hope that anyone reading this would consider others and take their habit outside so as not to smell up the house.

Shopping

A man was shopping for a shirt and found a beautiful cotton one that he liked, but when he found

TAKE UP A HOBBY

out it had to be ironed, he didn't take it. "My wife does not like to iron," he said. So? Why doesn't he iron it himself? Some men do. It's not just a woman thing to iron. Look at the dry cleaners and the tailors—mostly men—and they iron, sew, etc. Professional bakers are mostly men too. So why not bake breads, cookies, cakes? It's fun. Try it. You might like it. However, don't be like the one who gets every dish and pan out of the cupboard and then leaves a mess to clean up. Or like the one who started his cooking debut with some gourmet dish that used yak butter and pheasant eggs. How did I get on this subject? But since I am here, let me request that you do not leave dirty spoons in the sink. Drop them in the dish-washer or hand-wash them and put them away. Also, watch when carrying water or coffee-ground containers so that they don't drip all over the floor. Unless you are the cleaner-upper.

Now, with that said, it's only fair to fill in the blanks with some stories and experiences that oth-

ers have shared with me. Of course there are two sides to every story or complaint, but I'll enclose them both and you can see for yourself where you and I fit in.

About Food Shopping

Do you know that I have been getting along, doing the shopping by myself very well all these many years? You have never complained, so why do you *now* think you can pick up the best products at the store? Yes, I am open to suggestions. If you have certain likes and dislikes, I want to hear them, but please, my dear, don't take over the shopping. I know you're only trying to be helpful, but there's a limit. Five different kinds of peanuts might be pushing it a bit. Believe me, I watch the coupon ads and the specials, and I buy according to our budget. So let's keep it that way; the economies really add up.

Of course, we can shop together and it can be fun. Perhaps you will find items that you'd like to try that I never thought of before. Let's talk about it—hey, we can negotiate, just like the big guys!

On the Other Hand (Others Have Said)

"My husband likes to shop. He's a better shopper than I am. He has

always bought the groceries, so I see no need to change that just because he will be around more. He even buys my clothes! It's fine with me."

About Driving

Do you know I have been driving alone since I was sixteen? And I have a pretty good record. And do you know, I have been getting myself in and out of the car and the garage without any problems for the past umpteen years, without your help? I appreciate your concern and your interest in walking me to the car, but trust me to back up into the street and lower the garage door without your help. Please try to resist the temptation to tell me how to drive. Just sit back and enjoy being a passenger once in a while. This includes advice on how to park. Okay?

On the Other Hand

"My husband is such a gentleman. He always escorts me to the car and opens the door for me. Then he holds back the traffic so I can back out of the garage safely. He's so considerate and kind."

Be Neat and Tidy

When you remove your shoes and socks, please don't leave them in the middle of the room. Put them

away—somewhere—in a corner, or preferably in a closet. Retirement does not mean laziness.

Smart Remarks

You think you're clever just because you're now a senior citizen! Not always so. Watch your tongue. Not everyone has a sense of humor. They don't always know you are kidding. Smart remarks to cashiers and waitresses are embarrassing, as well as pointing at your coffee cup for a refill, instead of politely asking for it. I don't want to have to always explain, "He's just kidding!" Be polite. Be a gentleman. Yes, you can be pleasant. Yes, you can joke,

but do it in good taste. No teasing.
And keep your hands to yourself.
Not everyone likes being touched,
slapped on the back, hugged, or
patted. There is a time and a place,
certainly, but not *all* the time and
to *everyone* on the street.

On the Other Hand

*"People understand when my
husband is kidding them. He has a
pocketful of jokes—one for any
occasion. I see no need for him
to shut down just because
he's retired."*

Television

I'm sure you can agree that it need not be on all day. Please! And thank you! And remember I have some of my favorites I want to watch too, so be tolerant. Agreeing on television watching is often a problem for us, but with the VCR's availability it makes it possible to tape shows and watch them later.

On the Other Hand

"We both like the television on all day. It fills up a void in the stillness."

Consideration

When I'm in the laundry room with the washer going and you're in the living room, or the other end of the house, don't sit there and shout at me and then say, because I don't answer, "You're losing your hearing!" I either don't want to shout back, or I don't want to have to walk all the way around to see what is so important. I'm sure you get this, and *I'll try to do the same.*

Try not to make corrections on the way I do things. I have a reason, a purpose, for clipping that piece of paper to the book page. Don't change it without asking because you think your way is better (I'll try to do the same with your things). And if you take something I've laid down and put it away, please let me know so I'm not frantically looking in all the closets, wondering what I did with it.

Speaking of closets: Please shut the closet door! Please shut cupboard doors and drawers. It doesn't take much effort to do so.

On the Other Hand

"My husband has worked hard all his life—since he was nine years old; I see no need to pick on him now. If he leaves stuff around, I just pick it up and don't scold him. If he leaves the doors and drawers open, I just close them. Poor guy, he deserves a little TLC. I'm so happy

to have him home, finally, that
I don't even mind when he clanks
his spoon on the coffee cup!"

And, How About Quiet in the Morning?

Remember when you worked, you left early and I spent a quiet morning alone, without noise, for many years? Perhaps we don't need the music or news on the television until we're up and awake. The news is not going to change in the next twenty minutes. Don't we have a station that says, "You give us twenty minutes and we'll give you the world!"? And they repeat the same stuff over and over again!

On the Other Hand

"My husband likes it quiet in the morning and I don't. But I try to keep the radio on softly so I can get the news without bothering him."
"That's not a problem for us. We both like to hear the news and soft music in the morning. It helps to wake us up."

Being Helpful

Yes, it's perfectly fine to put the washed clothes into the dryer, but let's first talk about heat temperatures and what should not go into the dryer, such as nylon undies. There are other mixtures that should not go into the washer or the dryer together. We'll talk and you can learn these household details.

Yes, I know how to call information for a telephone number or how to find phone numbers in the telephone book. But thanks anyway. Something you can do, how-

ever, is have calling cards made
with our address and phone number on them. If you're feeling
clever, you can make up some
interesting things to say on them.
Like: "Retired and looking for
work." Or, "Retired, don't bother
me." Or some really smart remark
you think up yourself.

Dress

A real no-no is wearing your old
suit pants around because they
won't wear out. Pass them along
to the less fortunate and buy yourself some comfortable casual
clothes. Polyester shirts, pants,
and suits are definitely outdated.
Give them to charity. Buy some

dressy casual outfits, something up-to-date, not left over from the fifties. And get some soft-soled shoes—like for tennis, walking, or jogging—something comfortable for everyday lounging.

Miscellaneous

- **You will not** *want to wear the same thing every day.*
- **You will not** *want to open the bed before it gets dark. (We are not ready for a casket yet!)*
- **You will not** *wear your slippers before five o'clock in the afternoon.*
- **You will not** *talk about all*

your illnesses, aches, and pains to strangers (they don't care).

- *You will **not** volunteer what your doctor said about your health (unless asked).*
- *You will **not** want to clank your spoon endlessly against your cup.*
- *You will **not** want to put your eyeglasses in your pants pocket with your keys and then get upset when they are scratched. Or when you sit on them and the stem breaks, you won't want to complain, because you will realize that you could put them in the case provided to keep them safe.*

- *You will **not** leave your coffee mug sitting around—empty, or full of cold beverage.*
- *You will **not** (please) rearrange my sewing basket or my makeup drawer. If it bothers you, tell me and I'll do it!*
- *You **will** want to close all doors (drawers, closets, and cupboards included).*
- *You **will** want to put lids back on pens.*
- *You **will** want to turn off lights when leaving a room or the garage.*

Am I asking for a perfect husband? Well . . . Why not? We all can strive for perfection, can't we? If we keep on trying, we're bound to accomplish partial perfection anyway!

Let's Recap What We've Been Talking About

THINGS YOU CAN DO

- *Get rid of accumulated junk—in the garage, attic, closets, cellar, or wherever.*
- *Do your financial homework.*
- *Keep up with house projects.*
- *Work on a hobby (something you've always wanted to do)—such as building models (trains or planes).*
- *Join the beautification*

committee in your neighborhood. Help plant flowers,
put up holiday decorations.

- Join the crime watch for your
  neighborhood.
- Teach in the literacy program.
- Go back to school, learn a
  foreign language, take art
  classes or computer classes.
- Mount photos in albums—
  like those vacation photos
  that have just been sitting
  around.
- Start your own business—an
  art gallery, used book store,
  a station for refilling fire
  extinguishers, a shop of
  some kind.
- Begin a new career—work in
  a golf shop.

We will both want to be up front with each other. Let's work it out. It just takes a little TLC and tact. I'll tell you what I'd like you to do and you tell me what you expect from me.

We can each write a list of things we want to do, including a budget for travel and living expenses. My list will include my usual routine for getting my hair done, meetings and activities that I participate in. Your list might include the same, plus other things you've been dreaming about. Make it outrageous—just as wild as you want, then we can see how we can incorporate it or tame it down to something we *can* do! If we're both flexible, we can work it out together.

Most of all, we will remember to have a good sense of humor and an even temperament. A hundred and thirty years ago, the Reverend James Bean wrote a little book on marriage, titled *The Christian Minister's Affectionate Advice to a*

HOME IS A REFUGE
TO WHICH WE FLEE

Married Couple. Some of his advice is still applicable today,

especially now that we are approaching retirement. He says

in reference to a "kind and amiable temper and deportment" that one should "seek the improvement of your temper at any price." And in regard to the home he says, "What will your house be without good nature? Not a home. Home is a place in which the mind can settle; where it is too much at ease to be inclined to rove; a refuge to which we flee in the expectation of finding those calm pleasures, those soothing kindnesses, which are the sweetness of life. *Endeavor to make your house a home in each other.*" Anyway, we'll be happy keeping the spirit of life and adventure going.

I hope this is helpful to you, my dear, and remember, I'm look-

ing forward to our even closer relationship when you finally come
home from your job for the last
time!

Your ever-lovin' wife . . .

About the Author

My husband took early retirement ten years ago, and to be honest with you, I was not looking forward to it. My biggest worry, of course, was having him around all day. Having no hobbies, I wondered what he would do with his time. My biggest fear was: What would I have to give up? Would I have to stop working? Being a writer, I need quiet time to think and create. How could I do this and entertain him at the same time? But I must say, his retirement has been a wonderful change for both of us. Every morning we take a walk, then he reads the paper and I work at my desk. Actually my writing has taken on a second life, has been better and more productive—perhaps because I don't labor over it as much. We have lunch, sometimes out, sometimes on the patio. Then he plays tennis or does some other activity—like picking up and sorting books for the Friends of the Library, planting flowers for our small community, changing light bulbs and such at his church, and I go back to my desk, or shop, or whatever I have to do. Sometimes it's to help him with things. (One thing he tries to do each day is something for the community, something for his church, something for me and our home, and something for himself—like reading. It has been working very well.) Our time spent together is delightful and fun and we are still putting in productive, full days. So far all is working very well, *and* we've been married almost fifty years to boot!

Advice only a loving mother can give!

Dear Daughter, About Your Baby • 0-684-87192-0 • $9.95
Dear Son, About Your Baby • 0-684-87193-9 • $9.95
Dear Daughter, About Your Wedding • 0-684-84836-8 • $9.95
Dear Son, About Your Wedding • 0-684-85968-8 • $9.95

FIRESIDE
A Division of Simon & Schuster
A VIACOM COMPANY

All available from Fireside.